MISFITS

A COLORING BOOK FOR ADULTS AND ODD CHILDREN

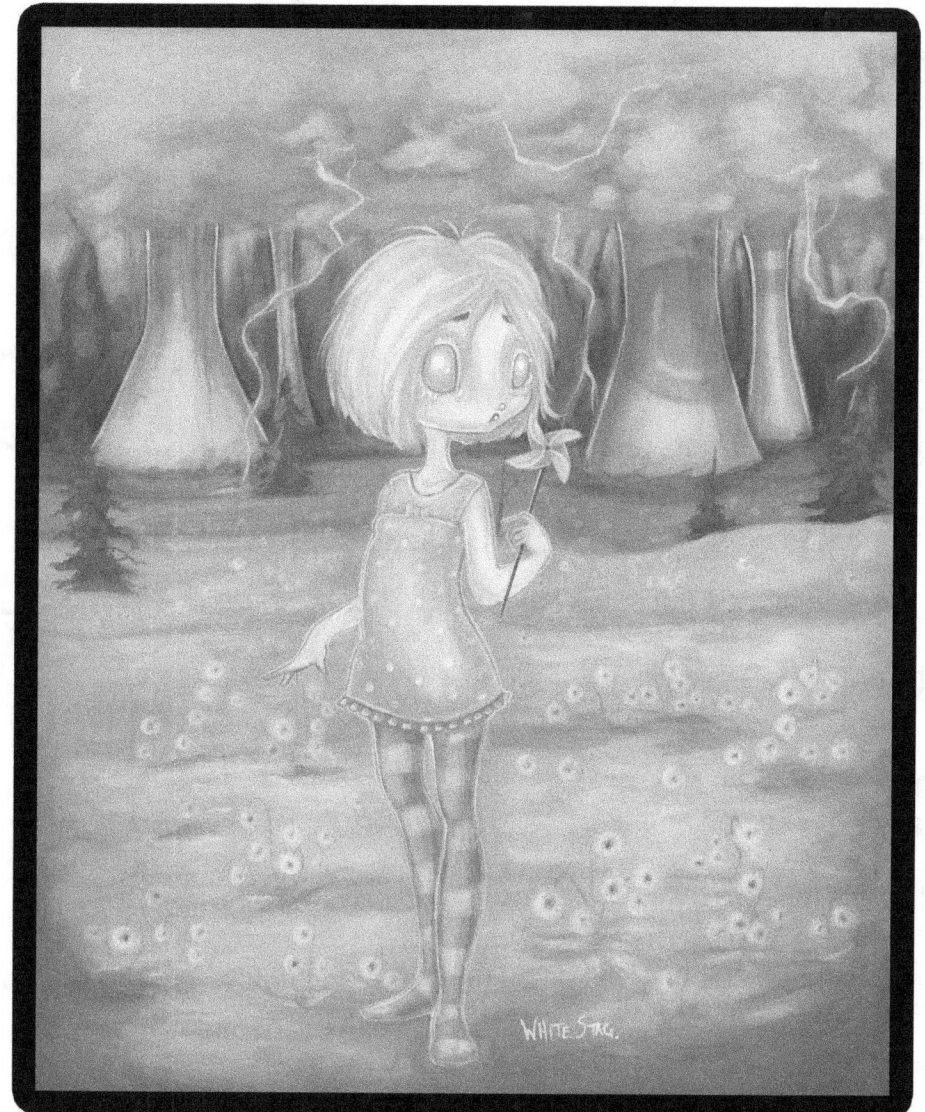

ART BY WHITESTAG.

No. 3

CREEPY CUTE WOODLAND CRITTERS, UNICORNS, HOBO PRINCESSES, DEAD GIRLS, ZOMBIES, PIRATES, FAIRIES, AND NUCLEAR FUN FOR THE WHOLE FAMILY! ENTER THE WORLD AND IMAGINATION OF WHITESTAG. MISFITS VOL. 3 IS A COLLECTION OF 25 IMAGES TAKEN FROM WHITESTAG.'S ART FEATURING A MEDLEY OF HER ART TO COLOR FOR ADULTS AND ODD CHILDREN.

ISBN - 978-1534961258

☆Helpful Tips☆

☆ When coloring always use clean sheets of paper between the back of the page you are working on and the rest of the pages of the book. It will help to avoid bleed through or indentions on other pages by accident.

◇ It doesn't hurt to have a test sheet for testing color schemes too. Sometimes colors may seem like they will look good side by side but seeing them first definitely helps.

☆ Always test pens and markers before using. You might find clogged or dried markers/pens can quickly ruin an image you are coloring and could make it near impossible to fix.

◇ Make sure to keep colored pencils sharp! The sharper the better.

☆ Don't forget to take your time, you'll get much better results if you don't rush.

◇ Remember, there really is no wrong! HAVE FUN! Spank it with glitter, give it a bow, or ignore the "rules" and color outside of the lines! Who cares, just have fun doing it!

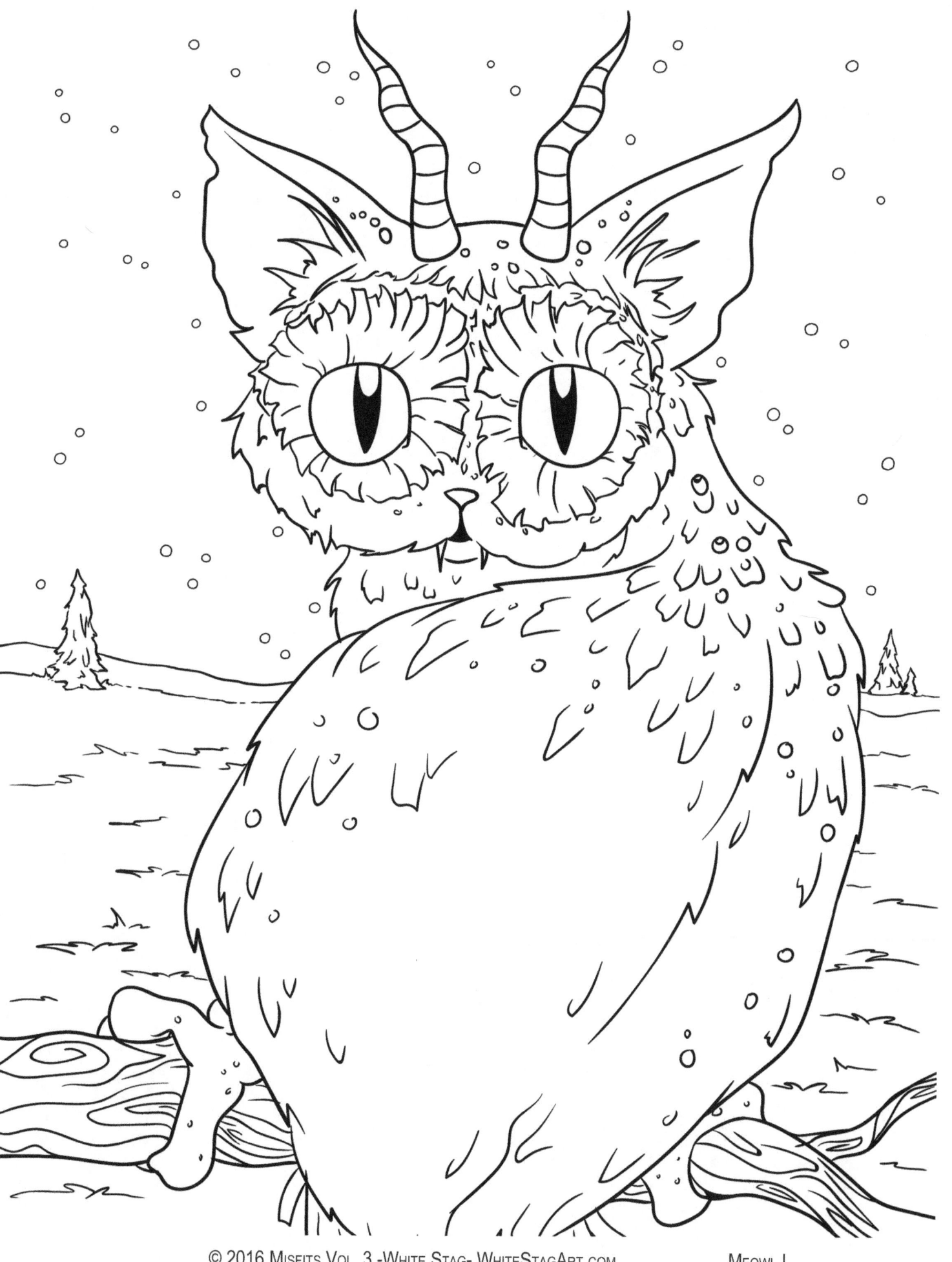

Meowl I

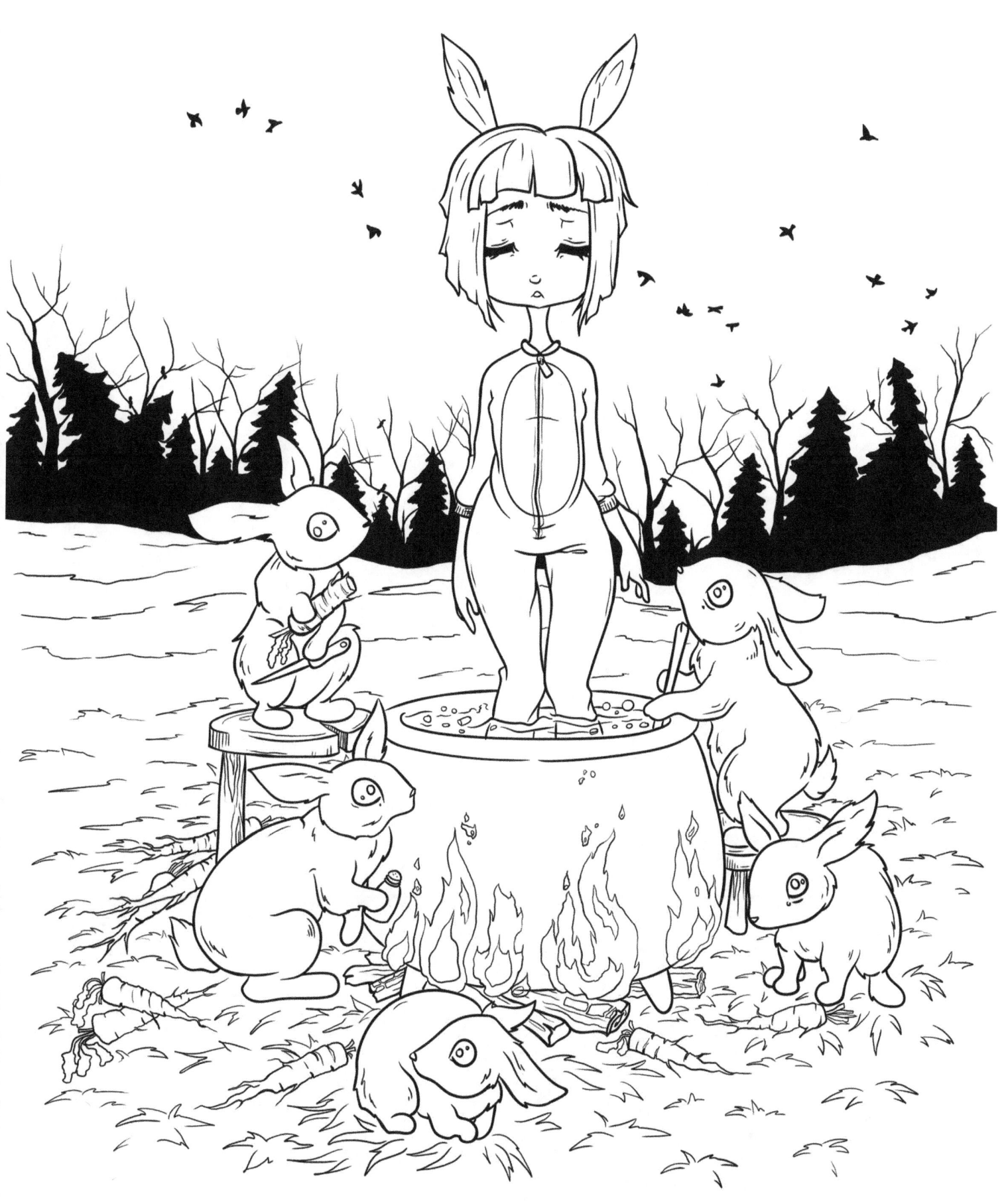

Rabbit Stew

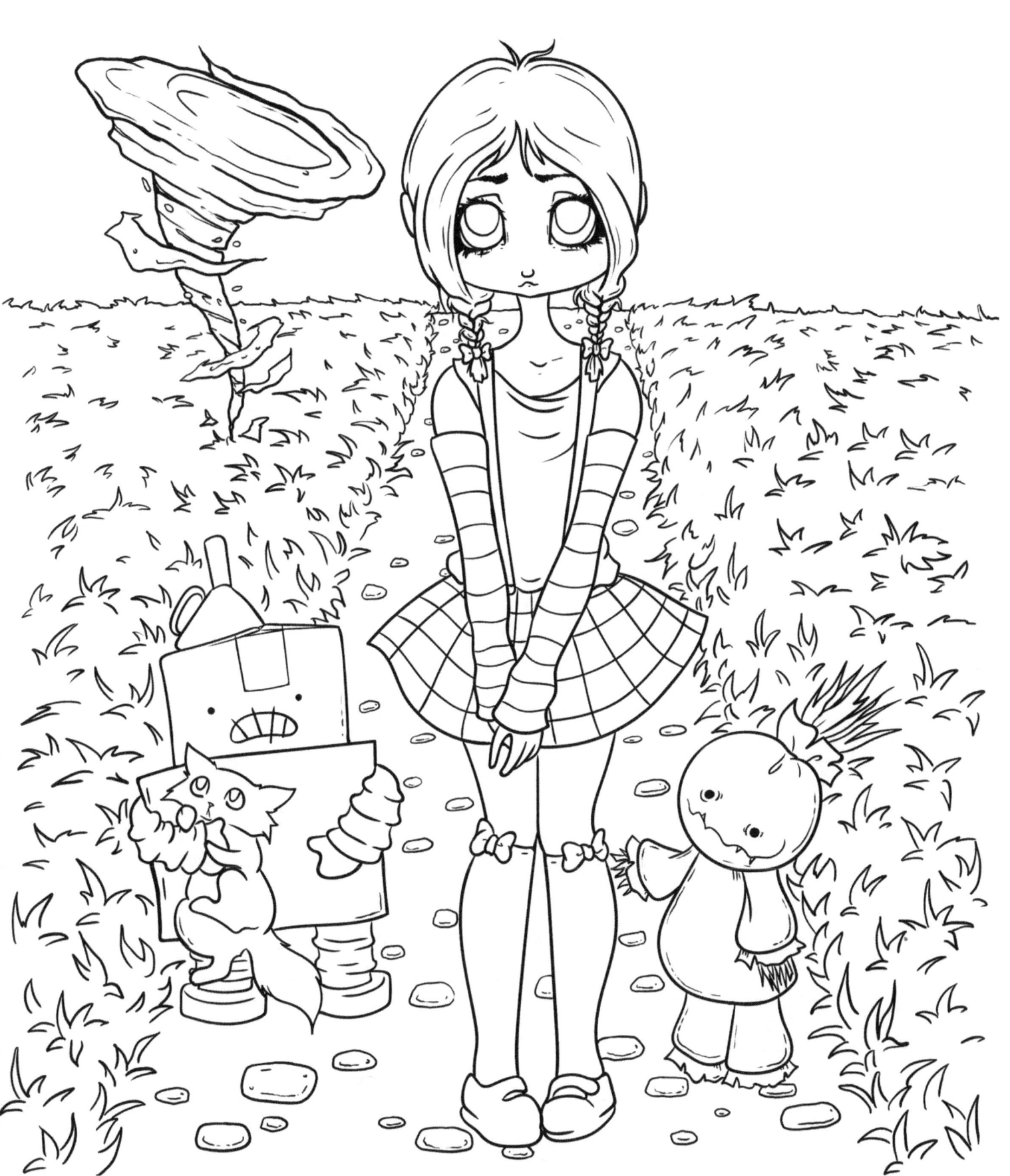

Oz

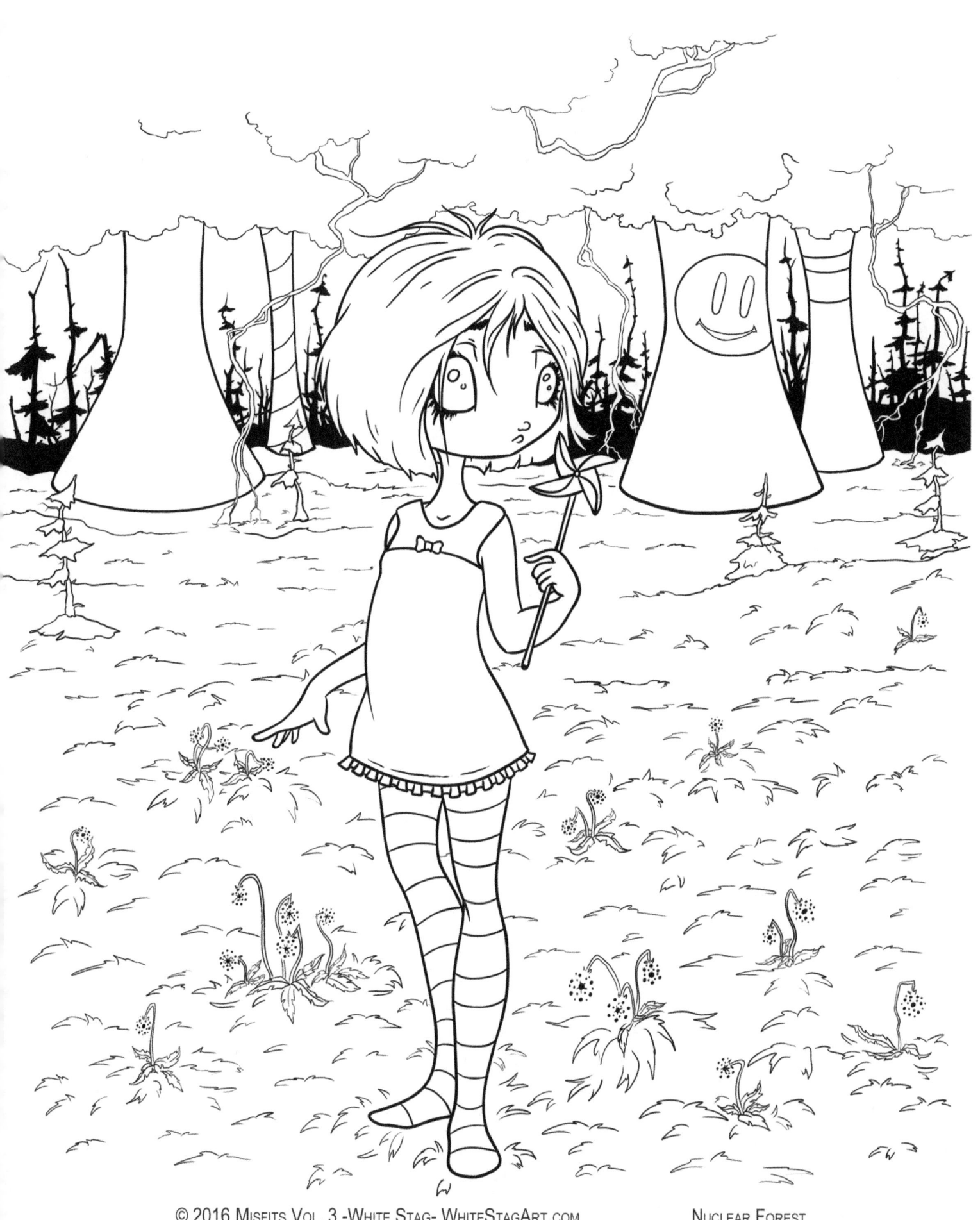

　　　Nuclear Forest

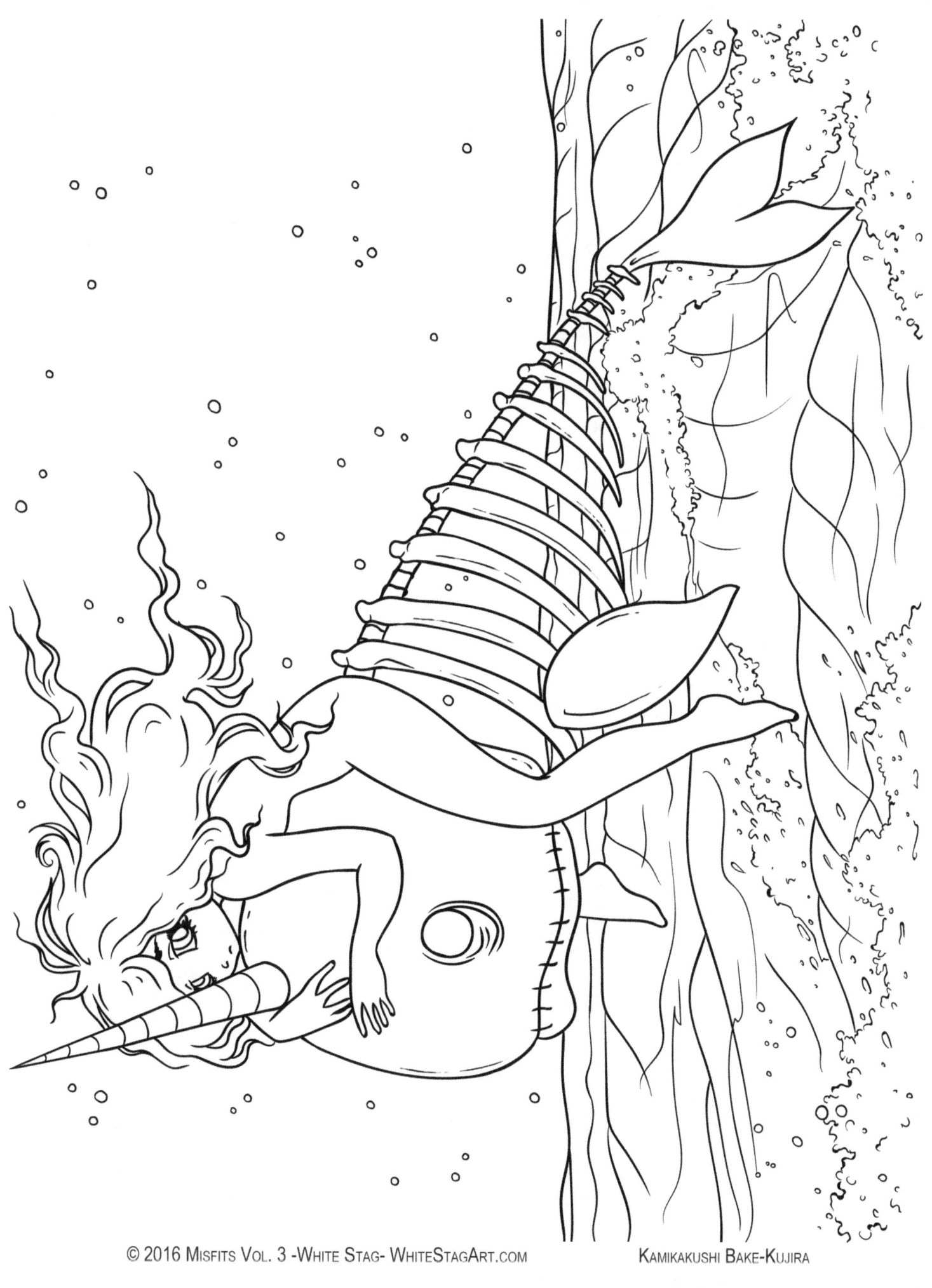

Kamikakushi Bake-Kujira

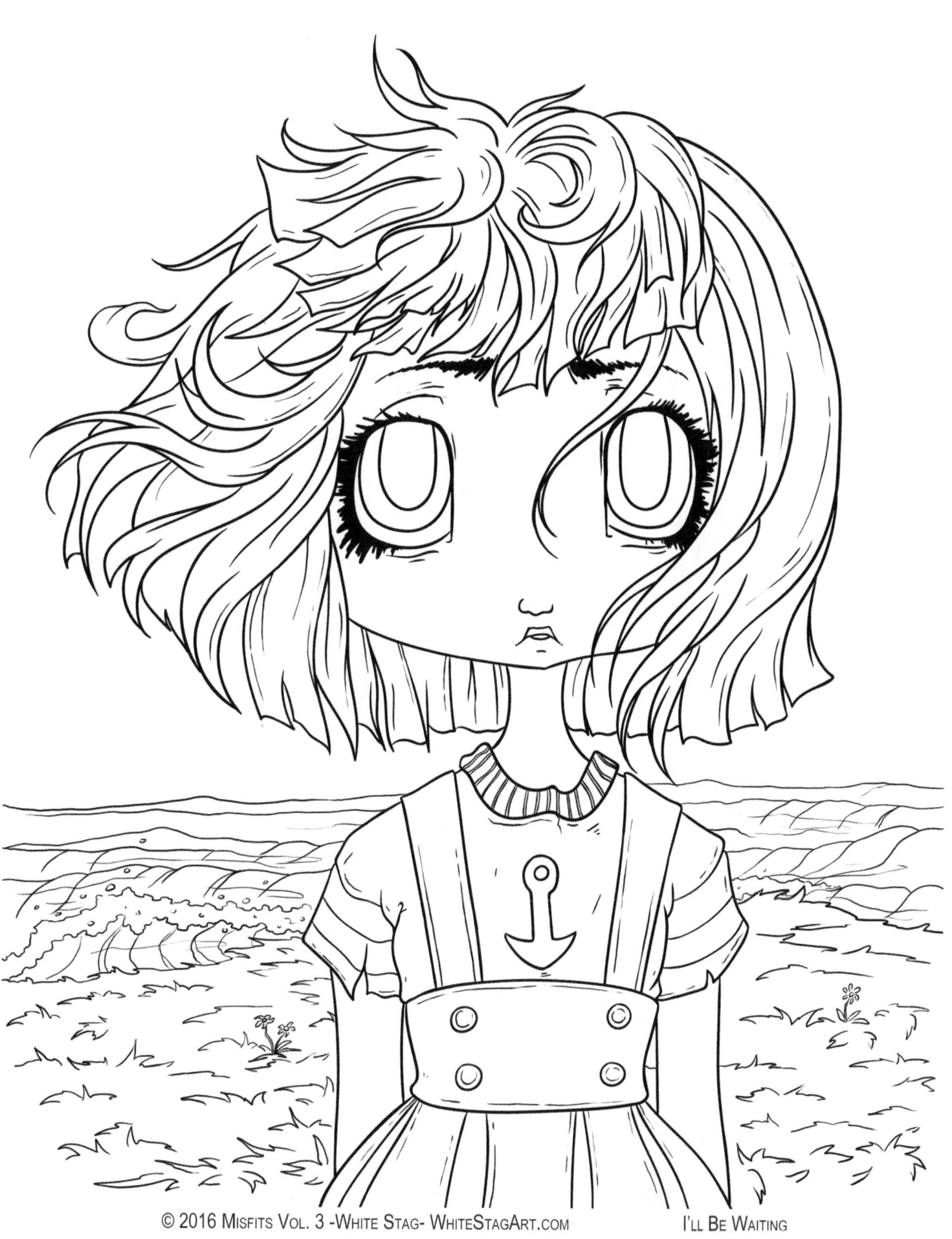

I'll Be Waiting

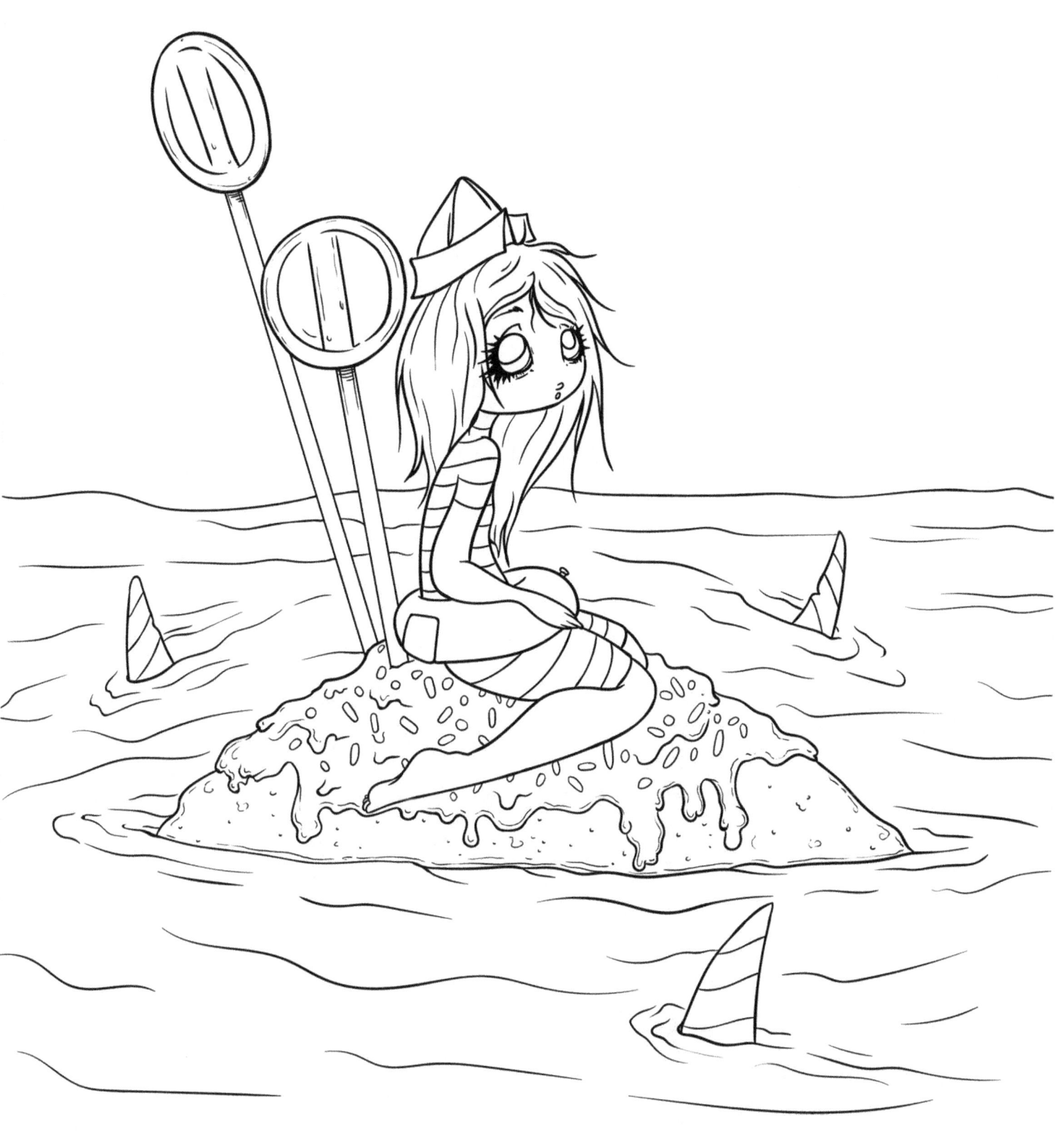

Desserted Island

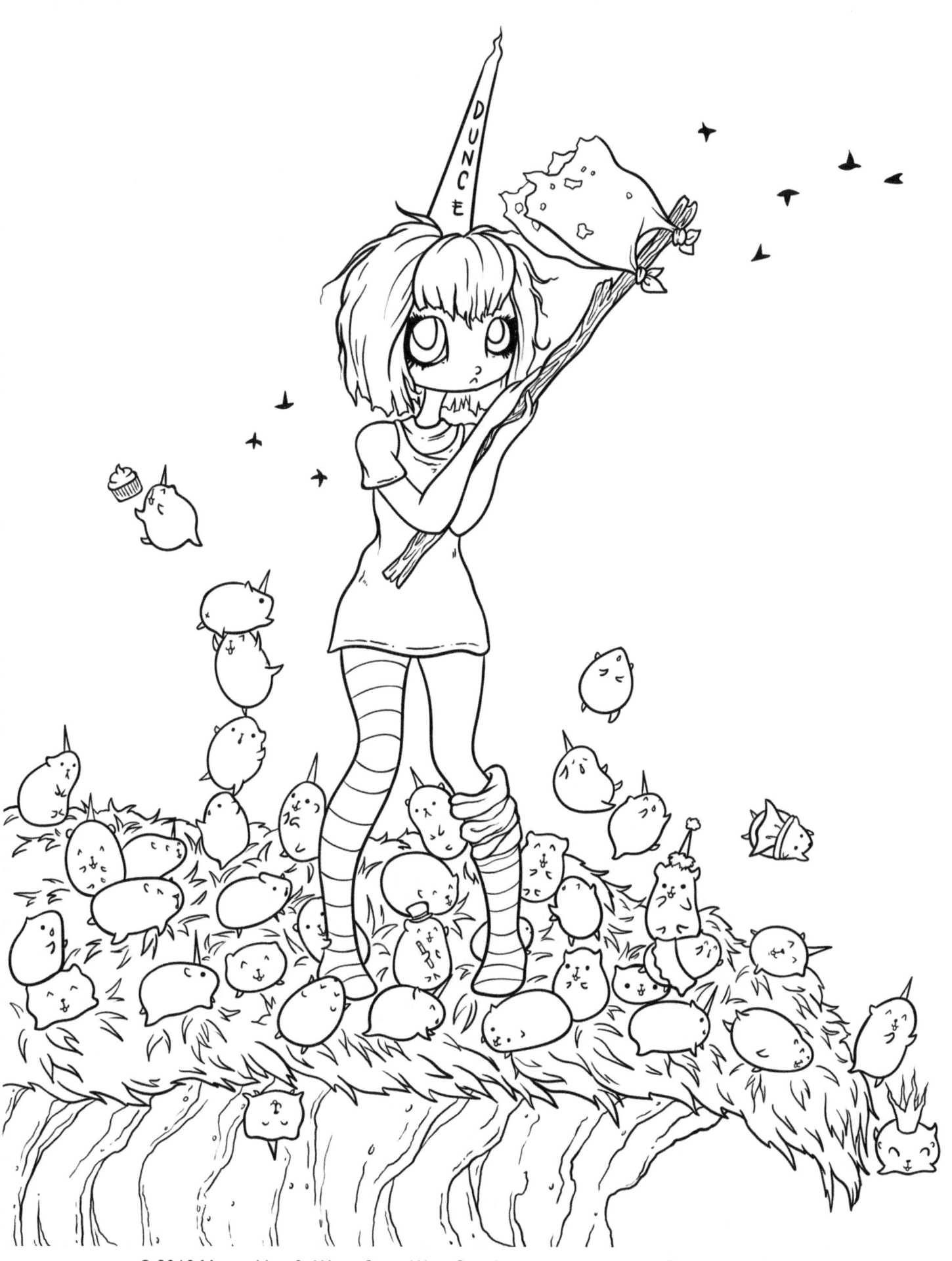

Dances with Lemmings

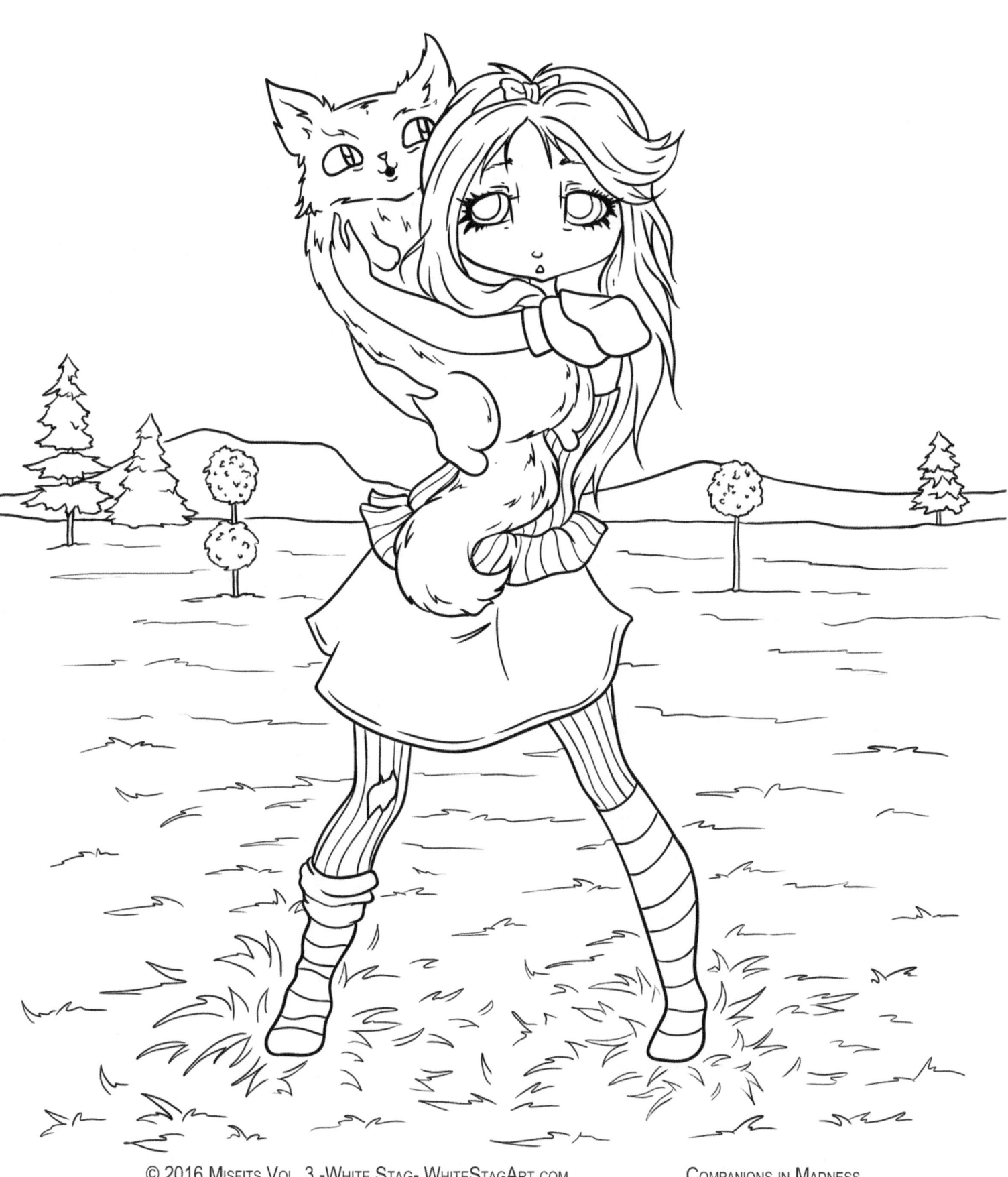

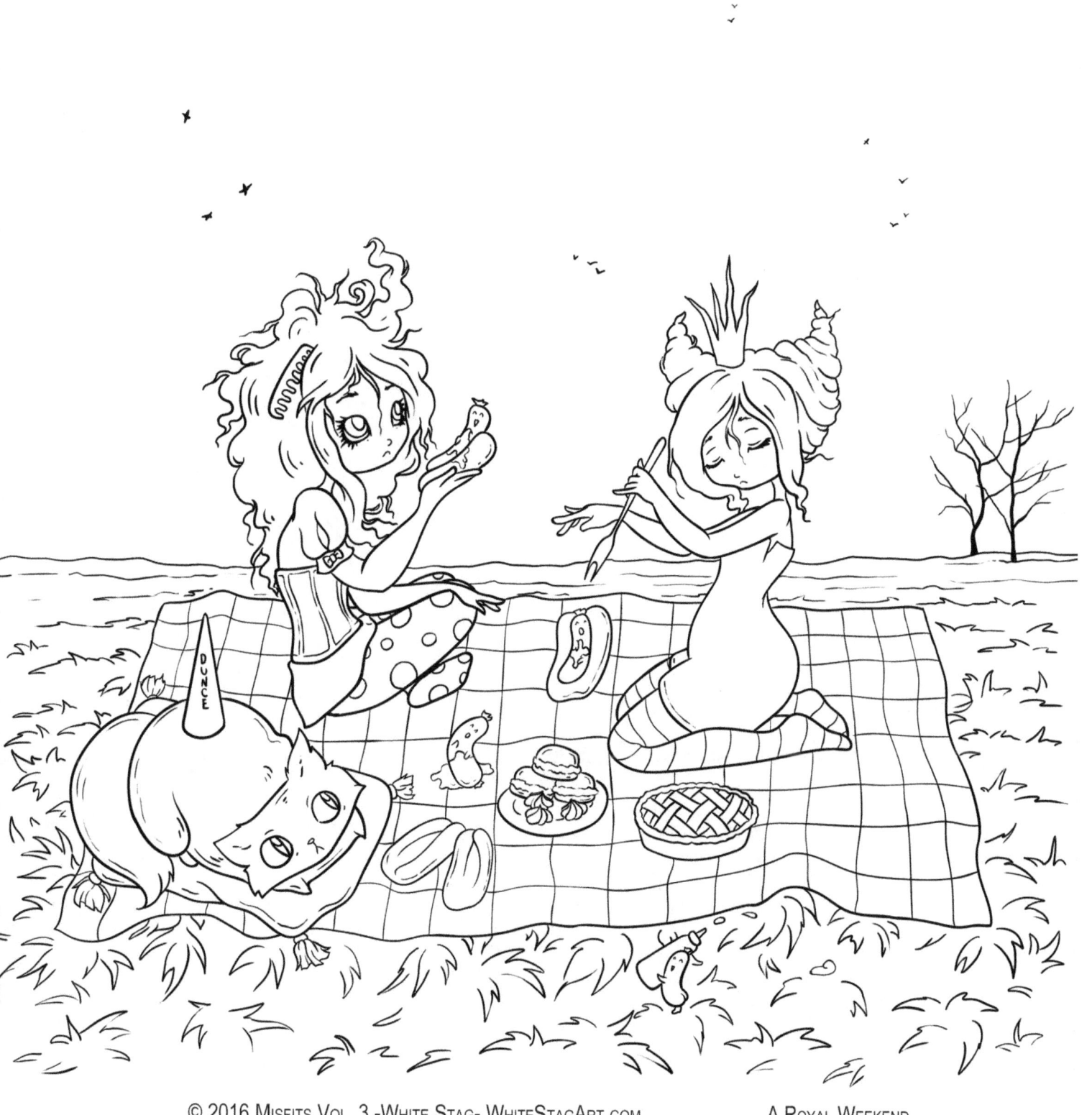

A Royal Weekend

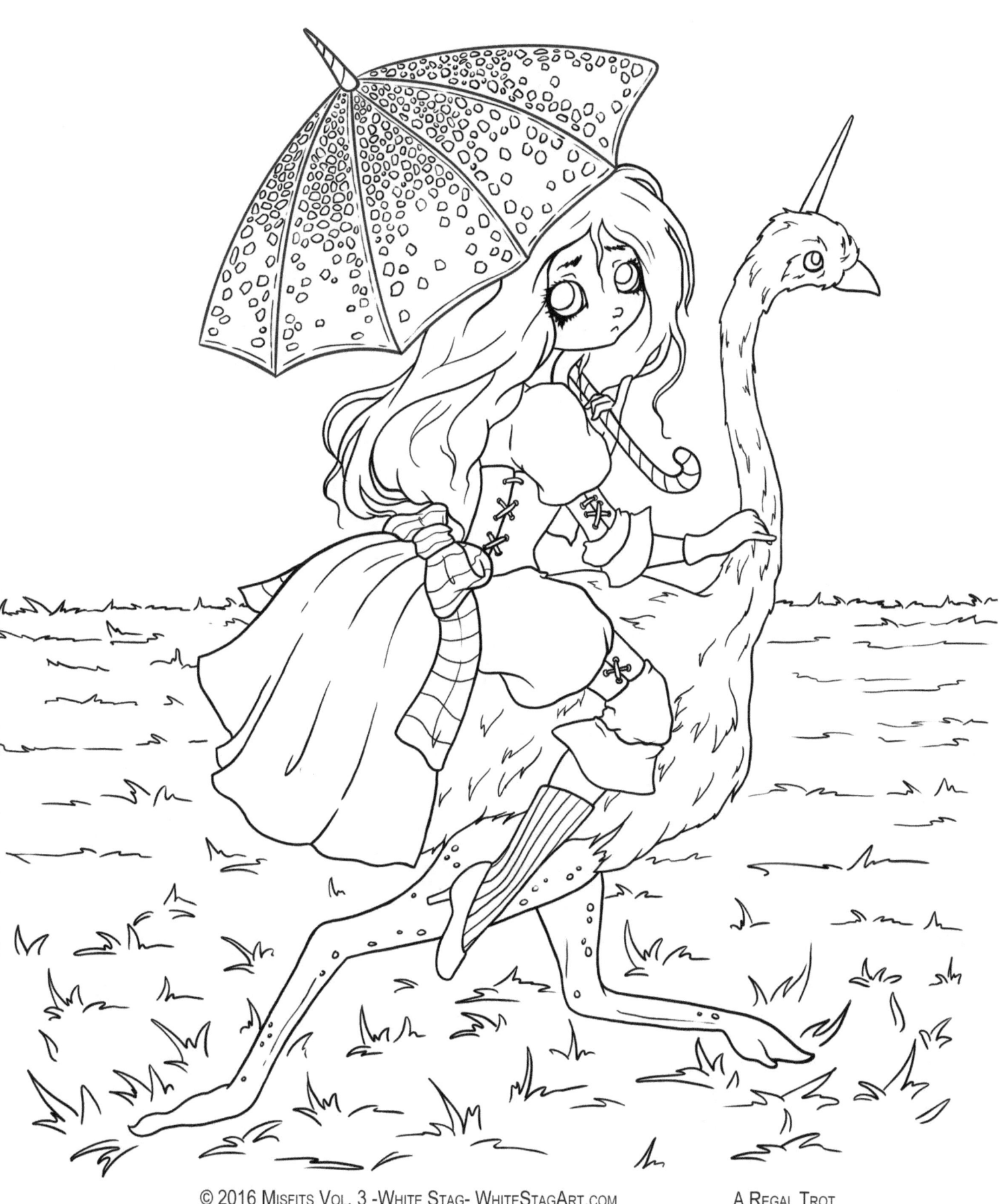

A REGAL TROT

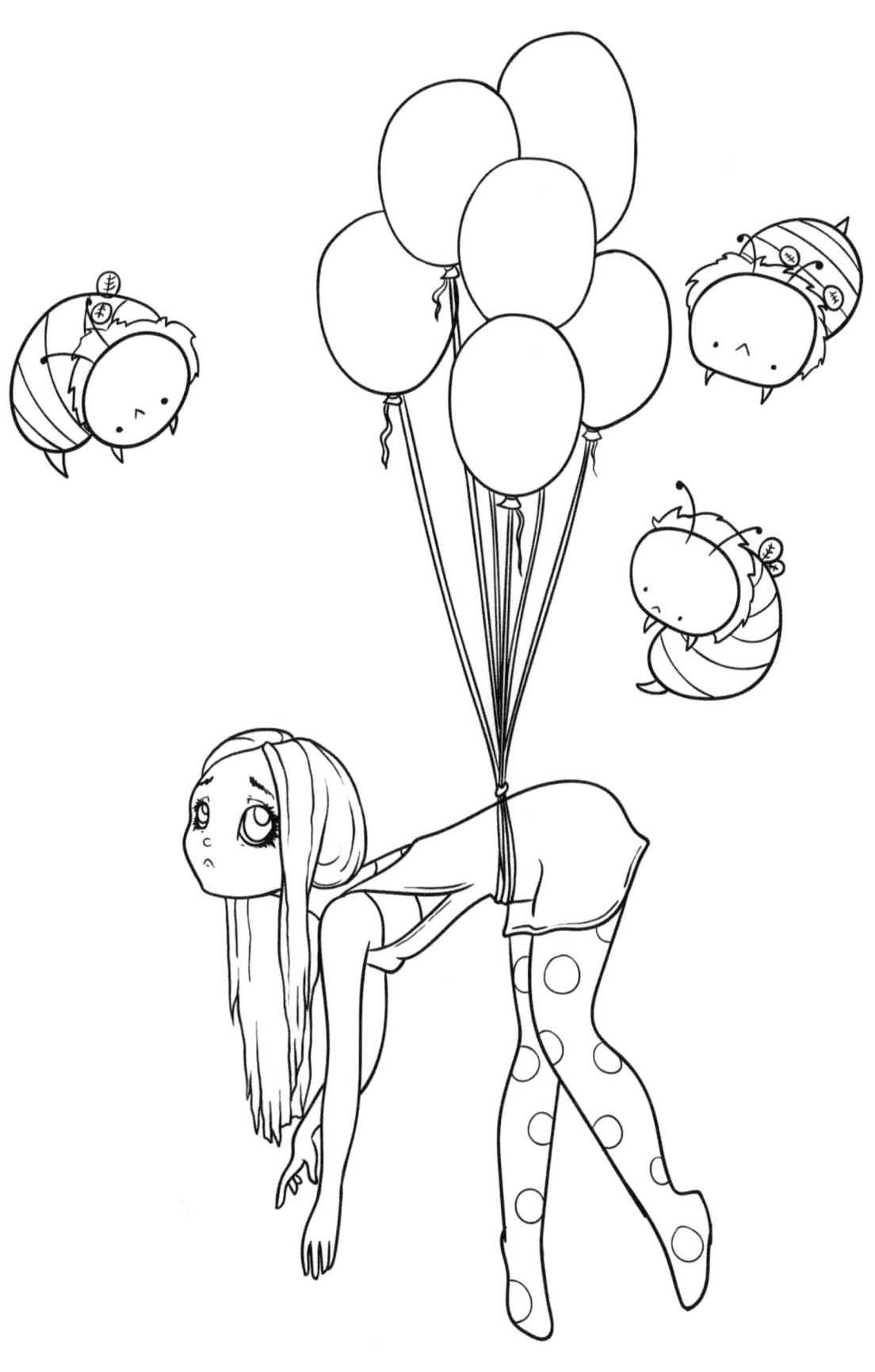

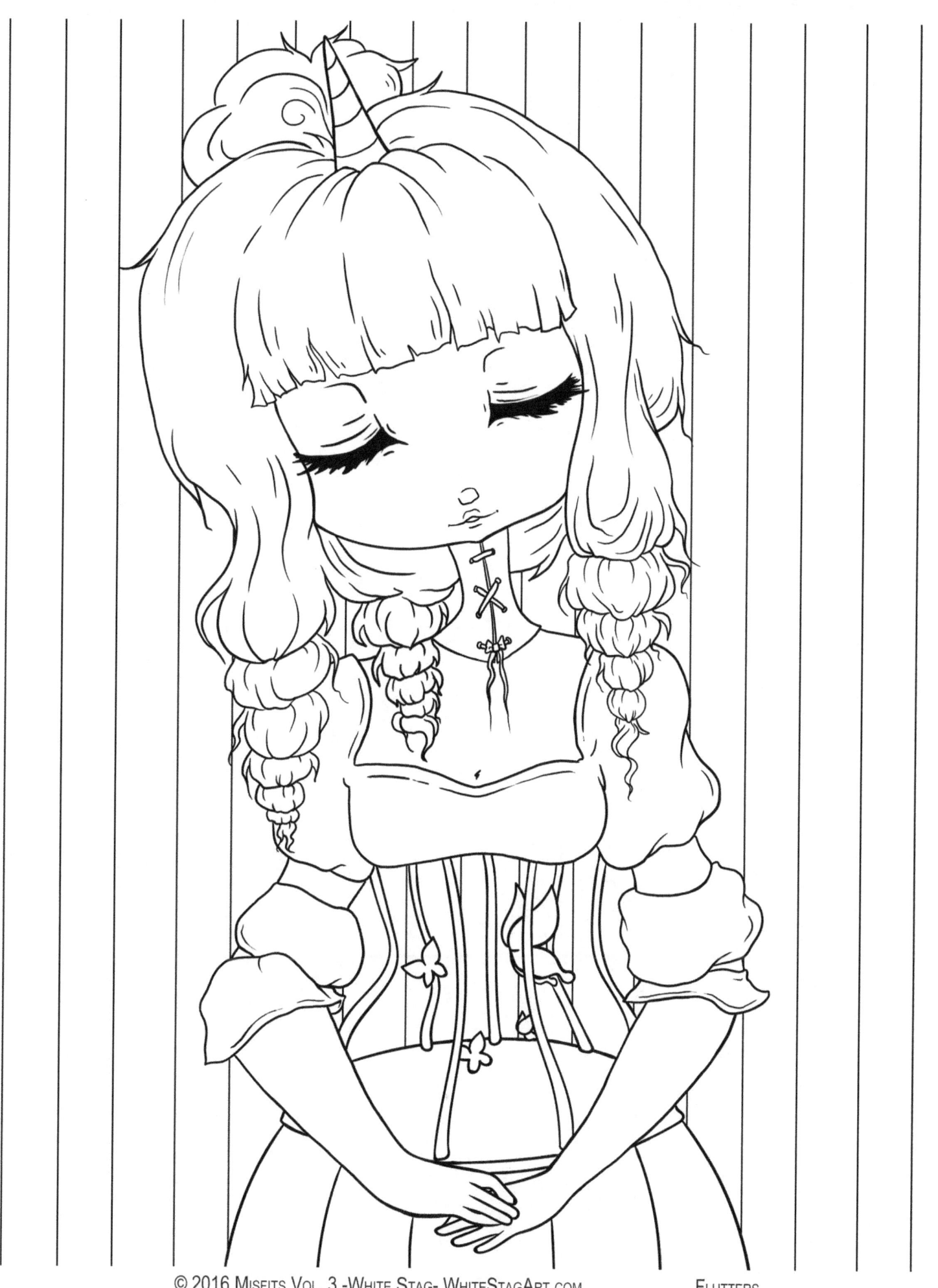

Flutters

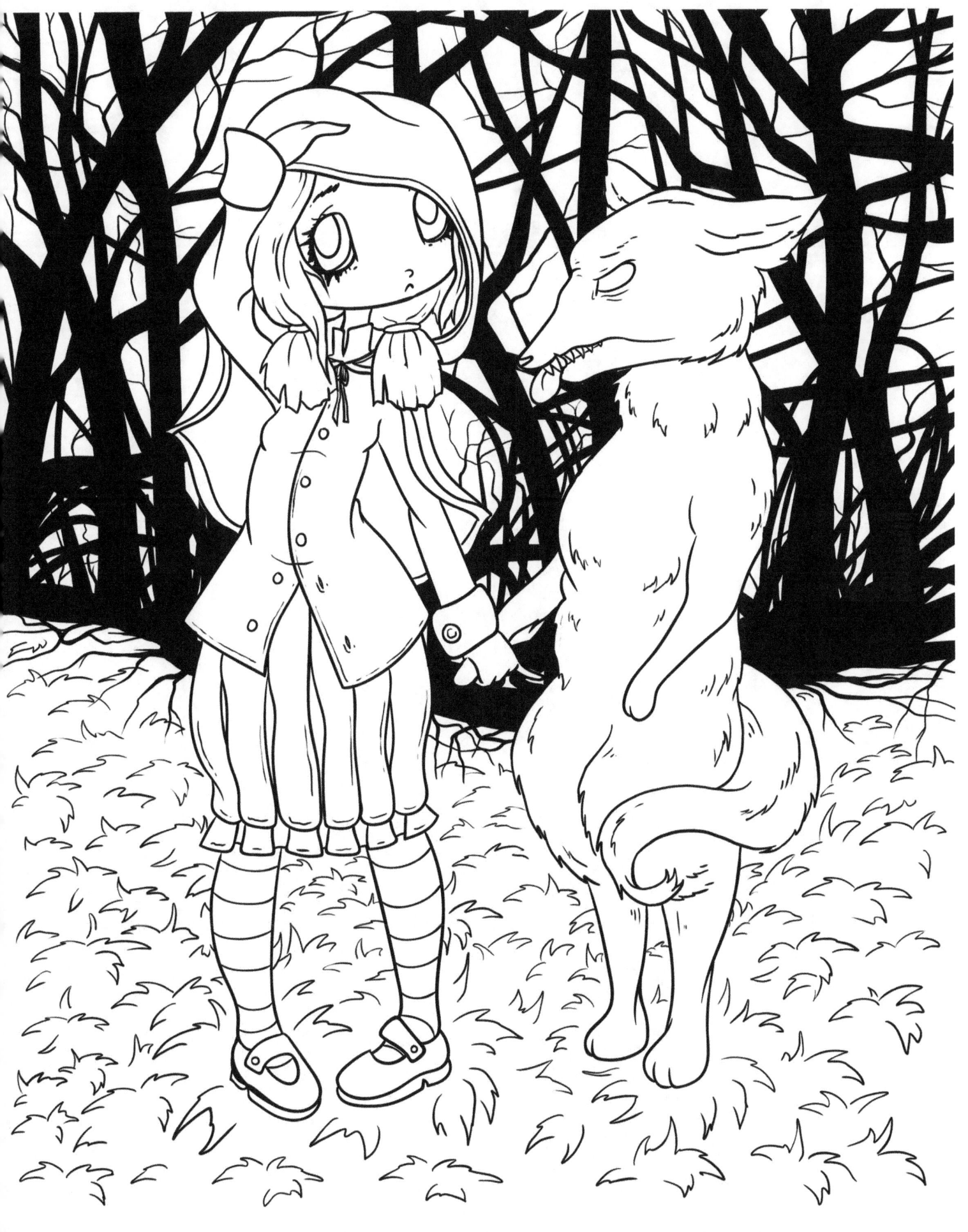

I Saw the Wolf

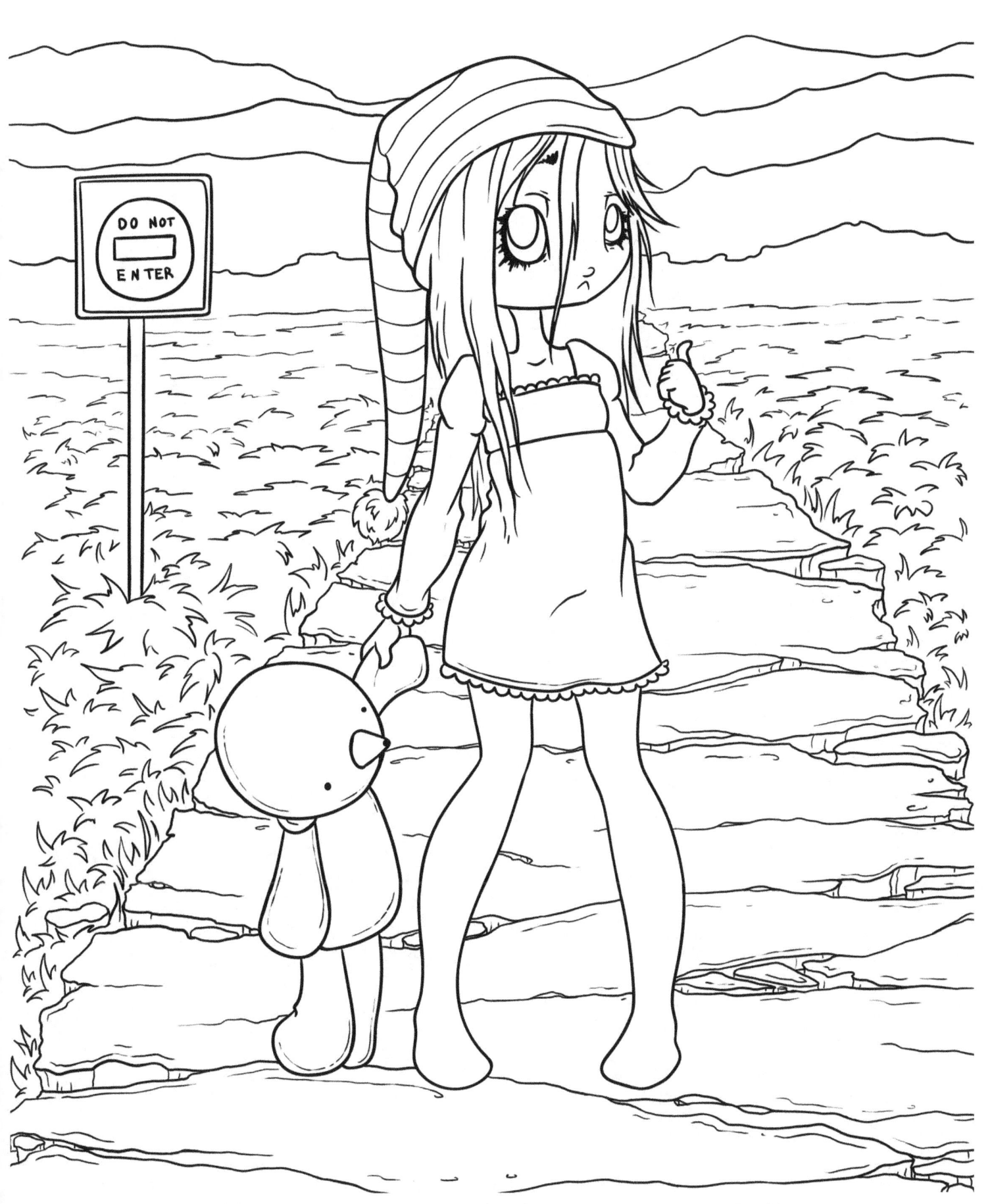

One Way

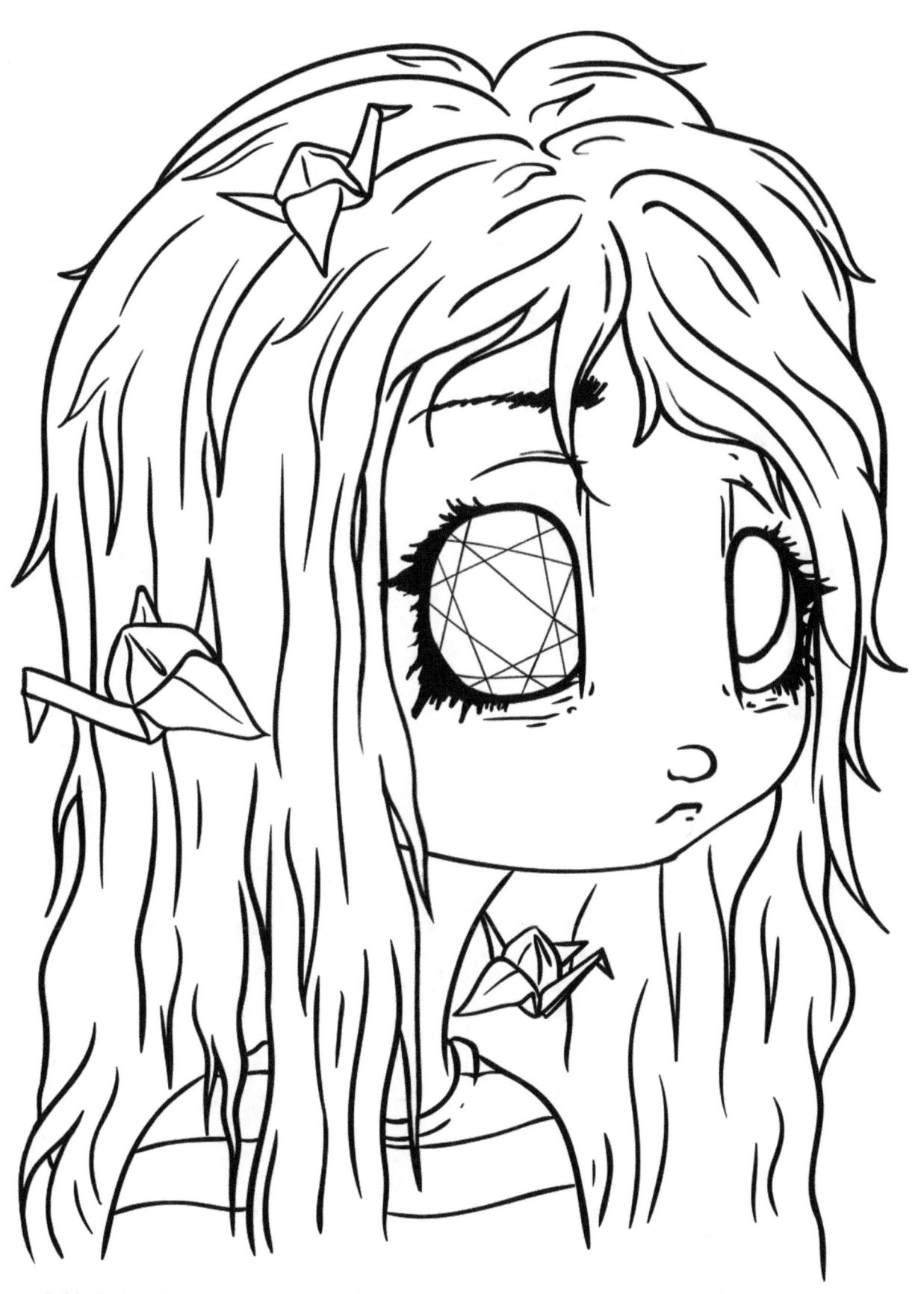

Stick A Crystal In My Eye I

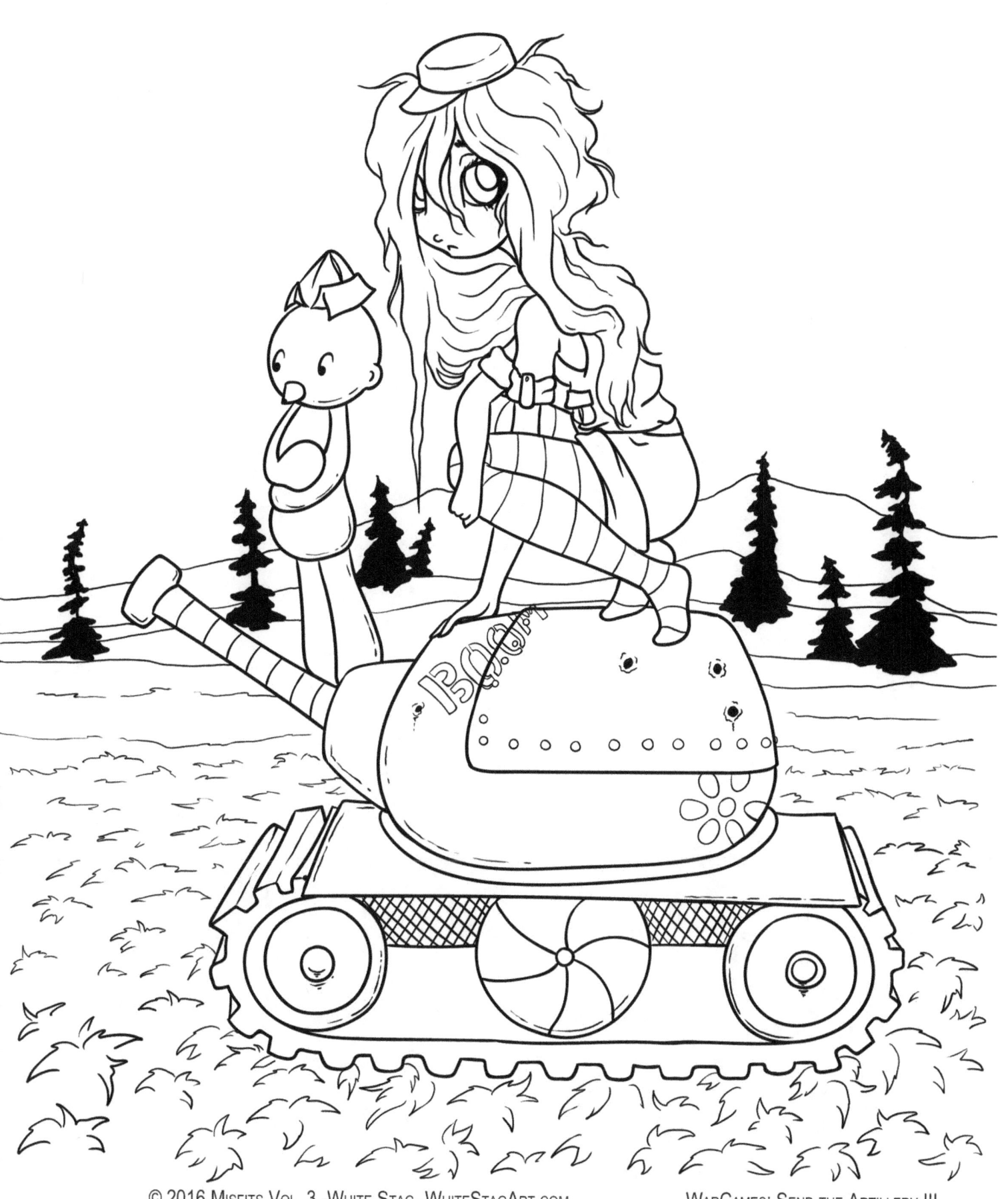

WarGames: Send the Artillery III

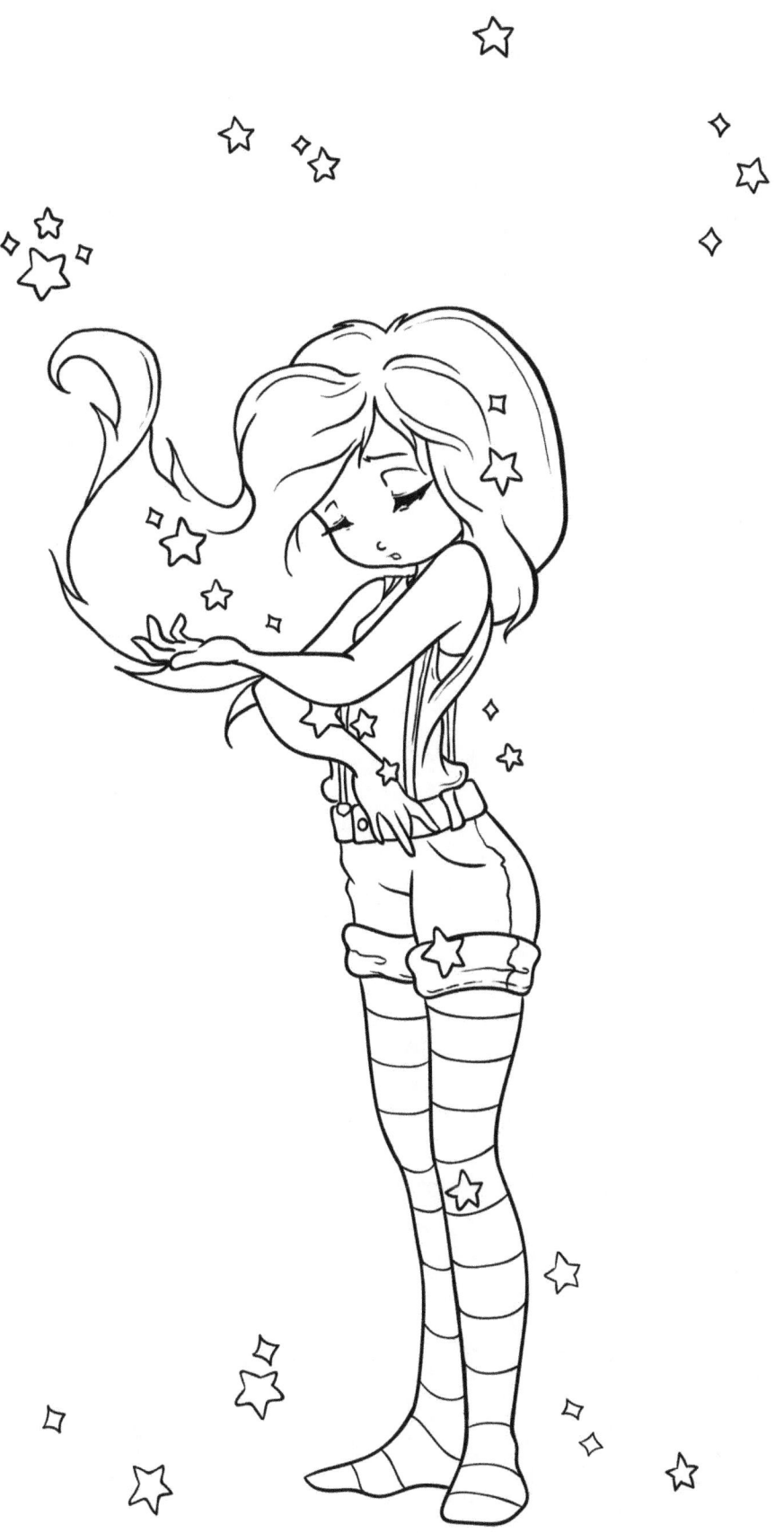

Twinkle

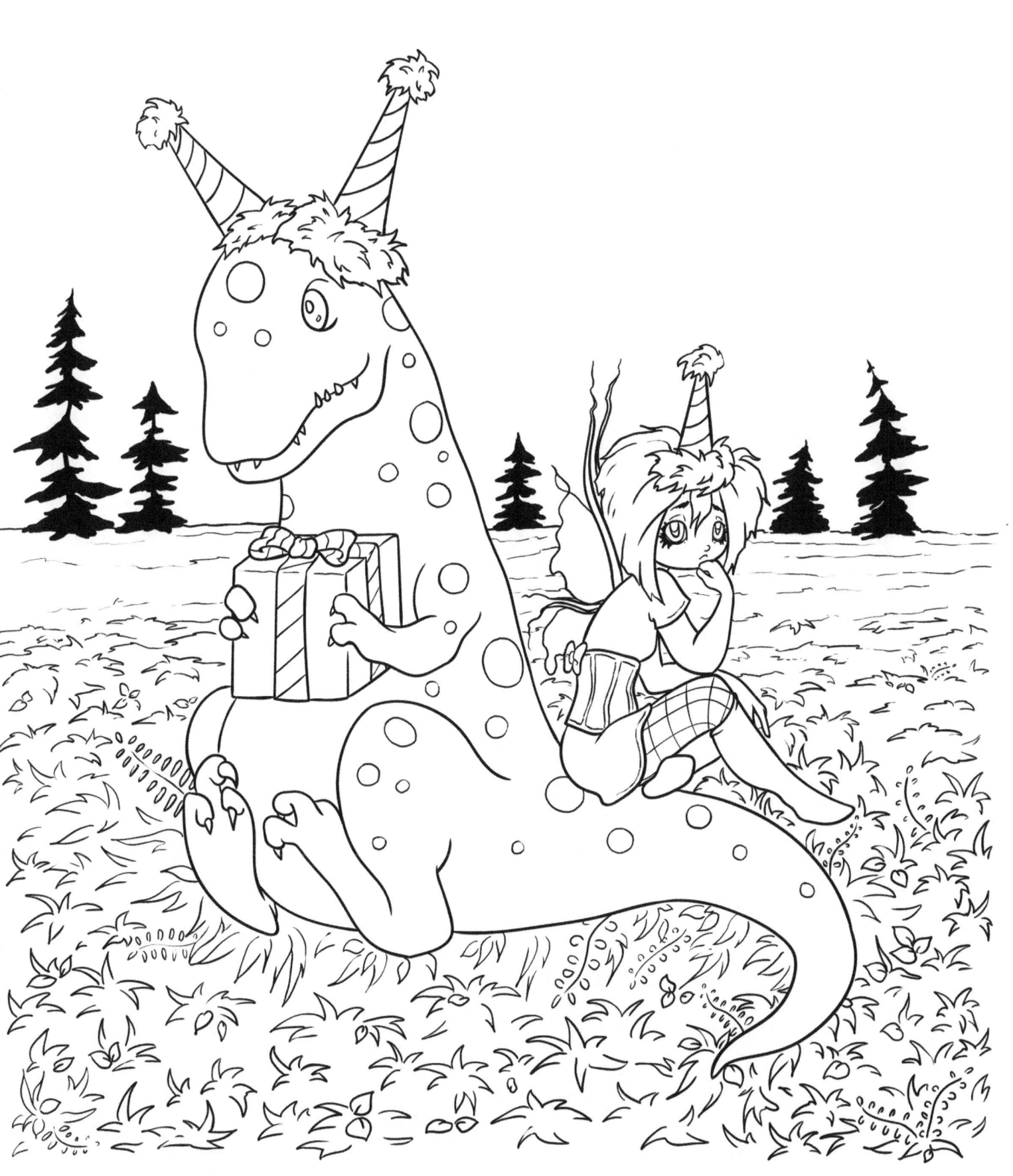

Trex Gets All the Presents

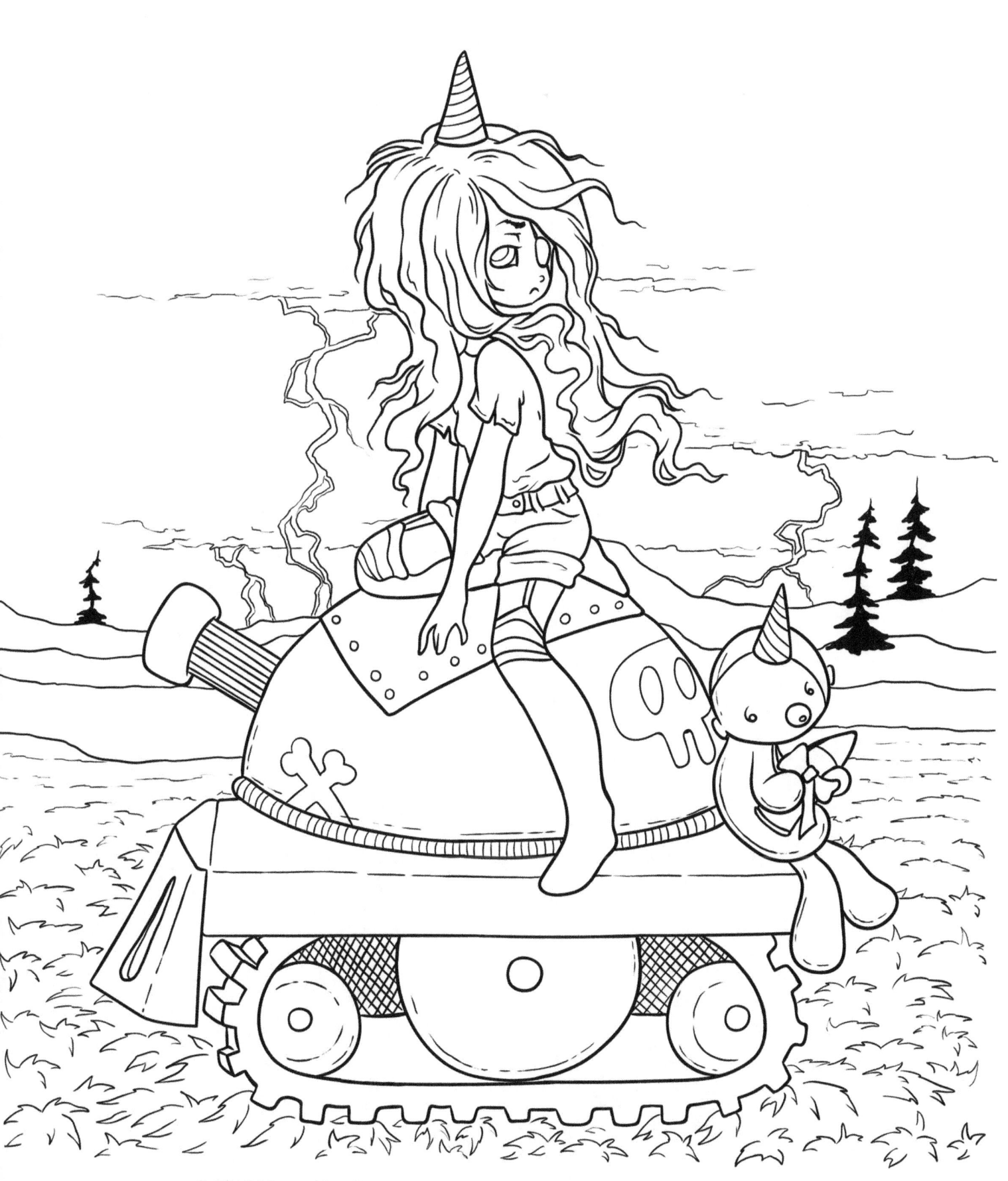

WarGames: To the Party

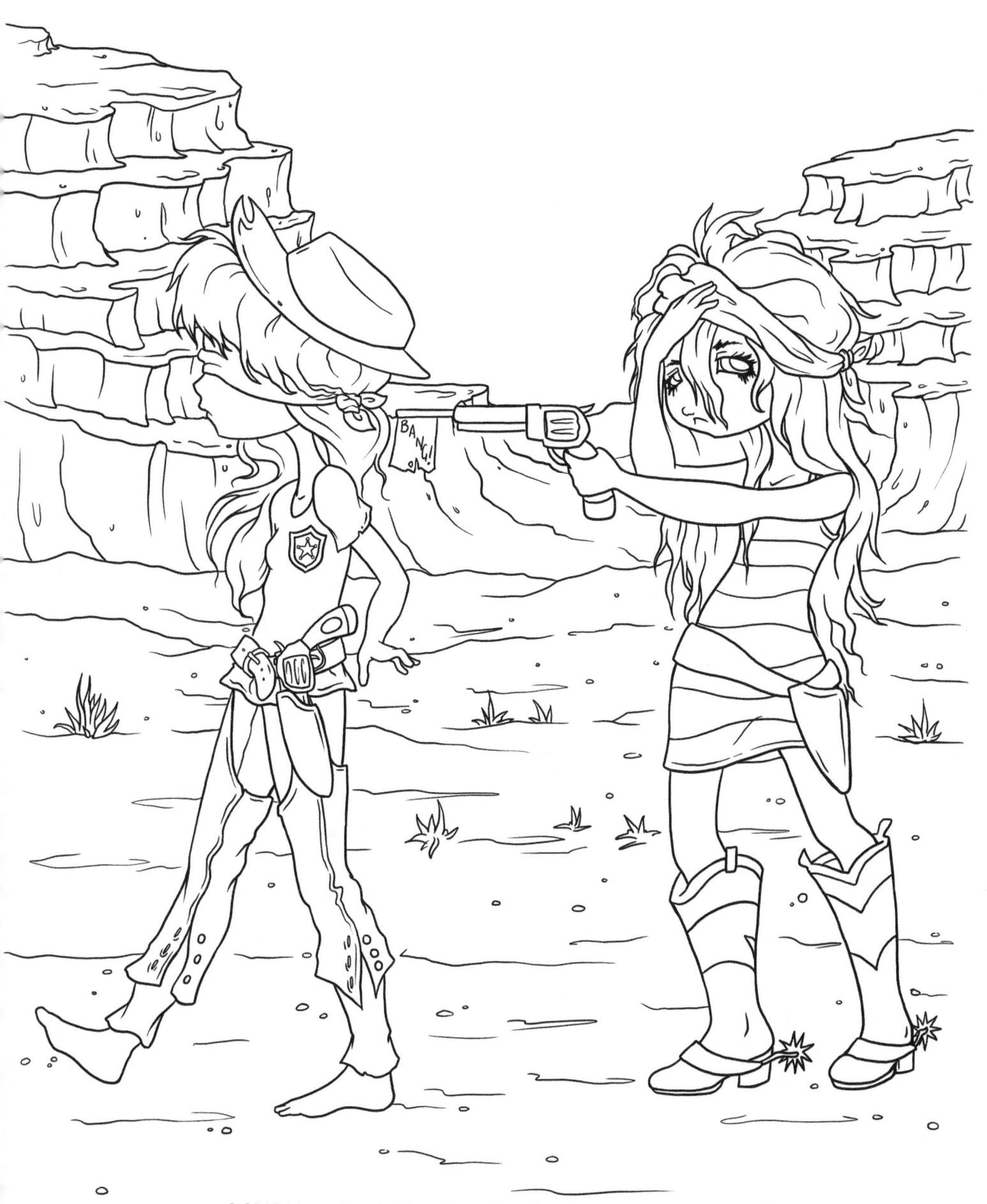

The Showdown

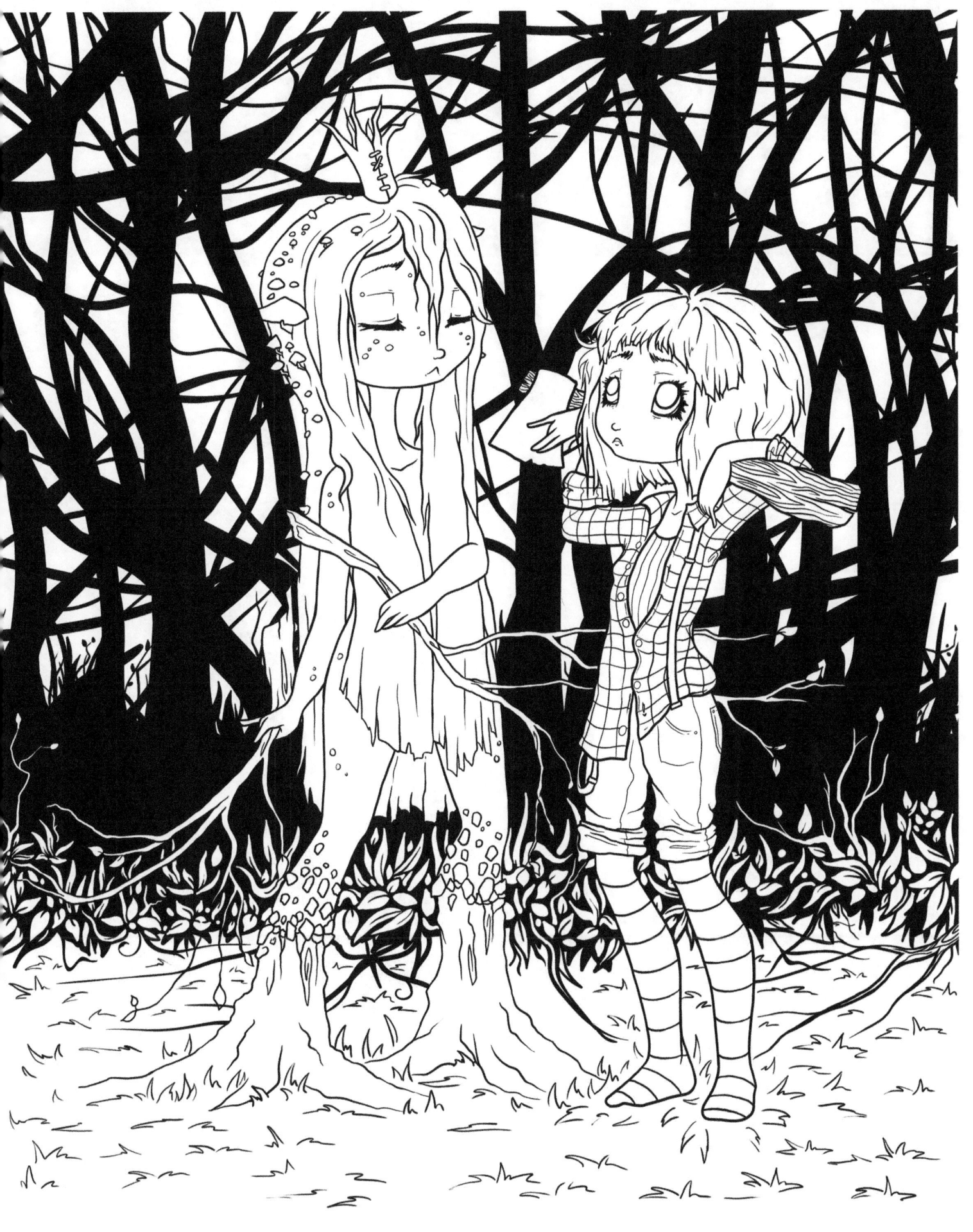

The Unfortunate End of Tree Girl

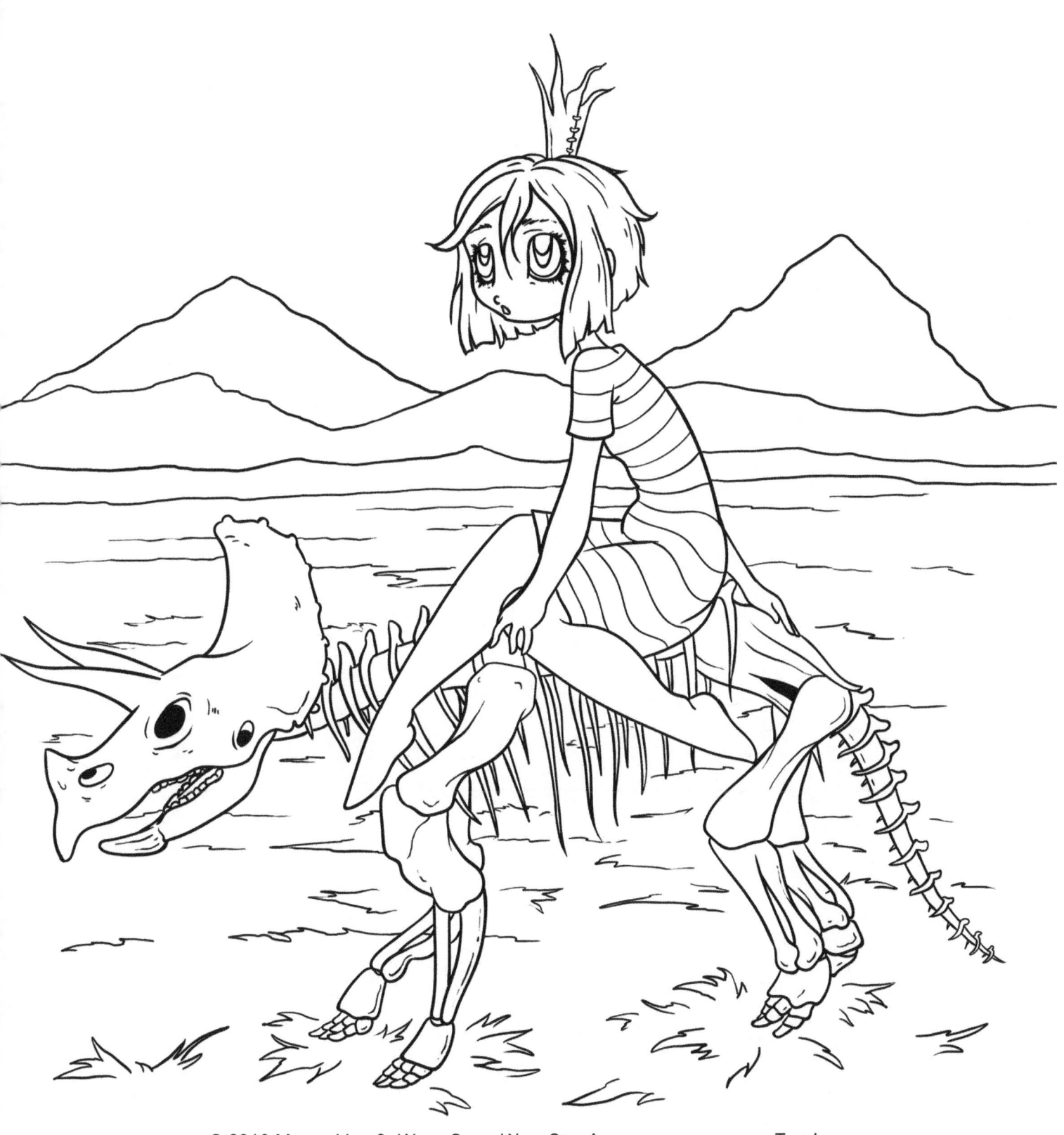

The Journey

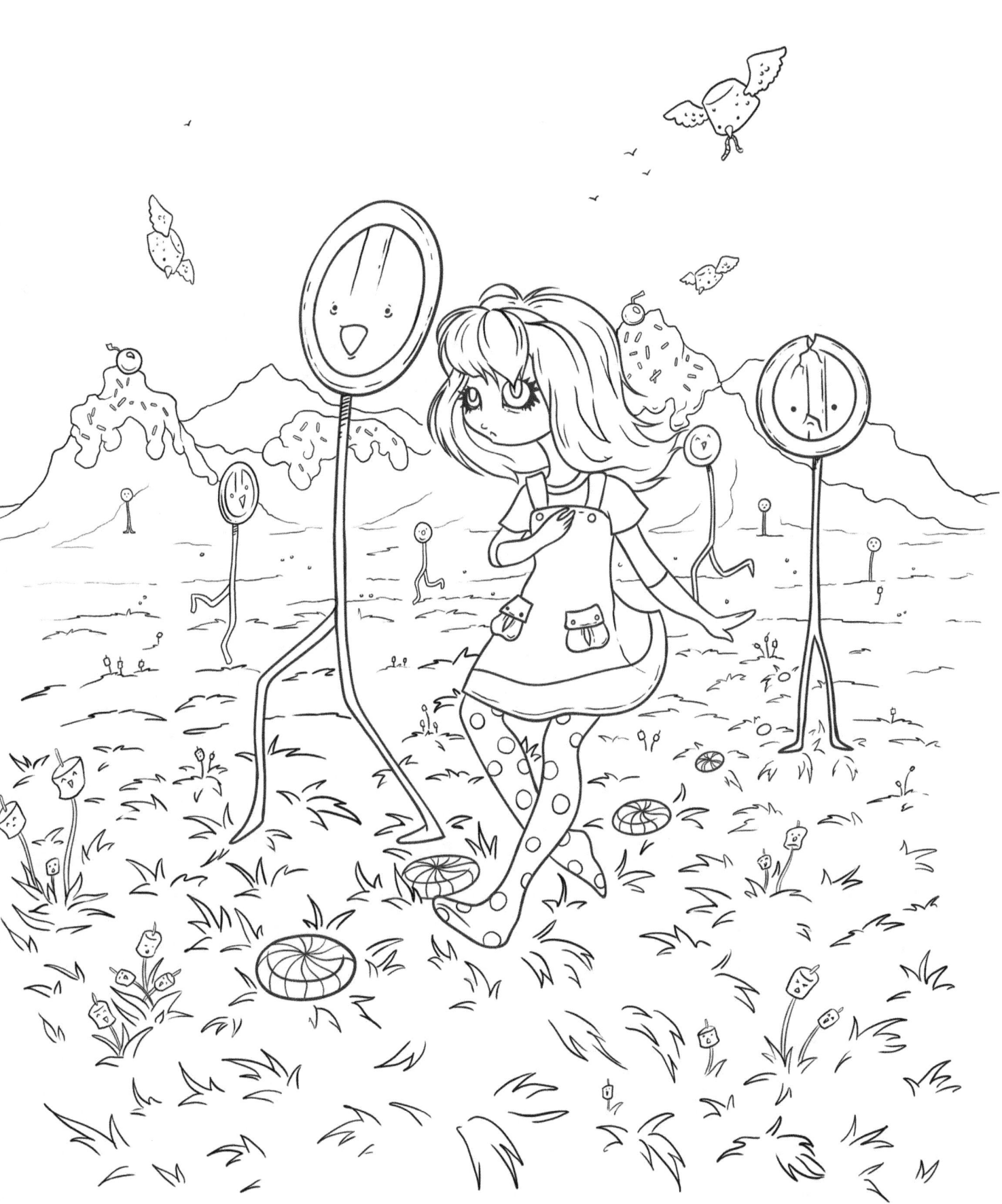

Sugar High

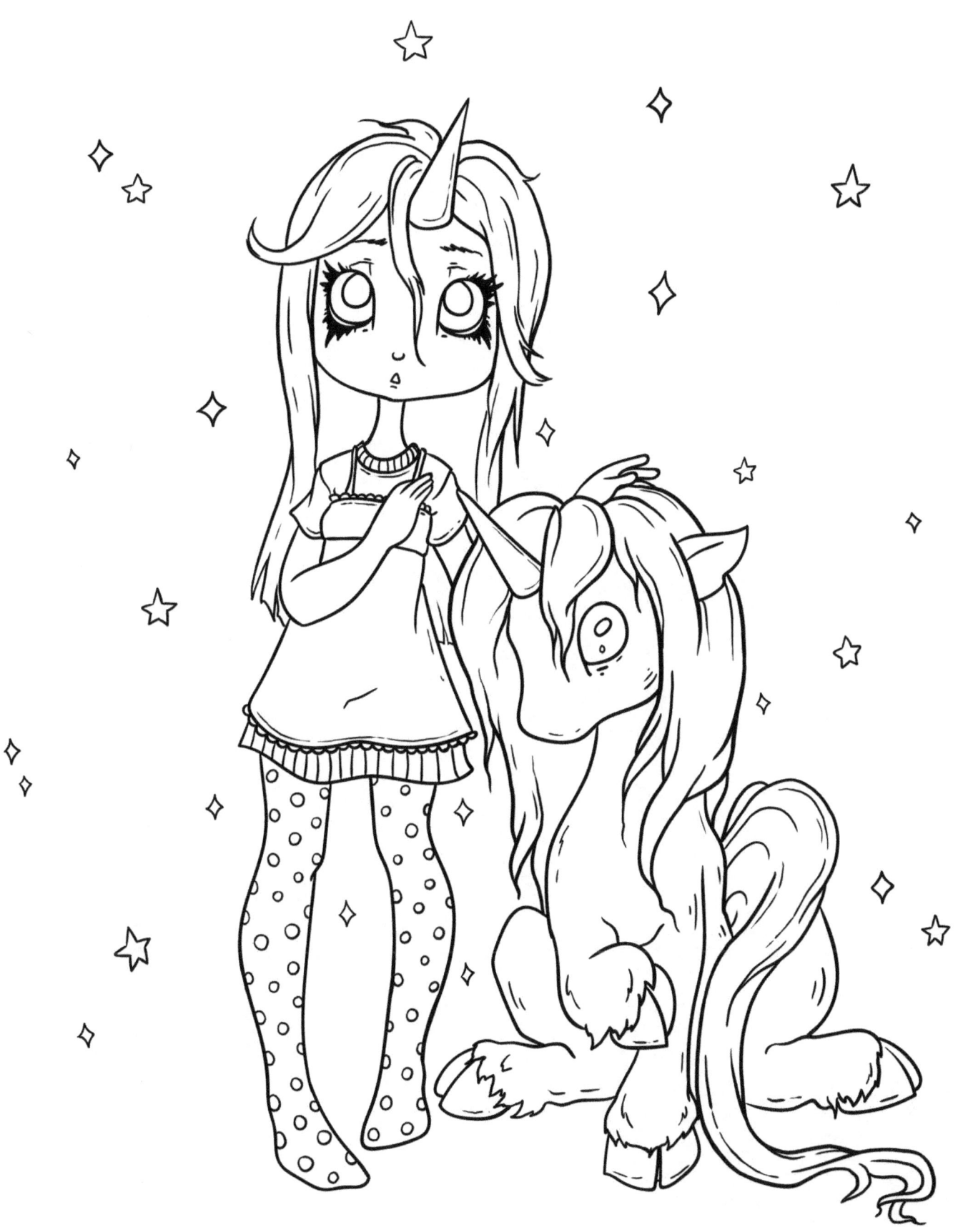

Somthing Sparkly

WHITE STAG.

THIS COLLECTION OF COLORING PAGES WAS TAKEN FROM MY ORIGINAL PAINTINGS OR CONCEPT SKETCHES I HAVE FOR FUTURE PAINTINGS. IN THIS BOOK ARE 25 BRAND NEW IMAGES FEATURING AN ARRAY OF MY CHARACTERS. I DID NOT INCLUDE ANY ZOMBIES IN THIS BOOK SEEING HOW THE ENTIRE LAST BOOK WAS ZOMBIE THEMED. I HOPE YOU GUYS ENJOY COLORING THEM AS MUCH AS I ENJOY CREATING!

MORE VOLUMES COMING SOON!
-VOL. 4 FAIRIES
-VOL. 5 NAUTICAL

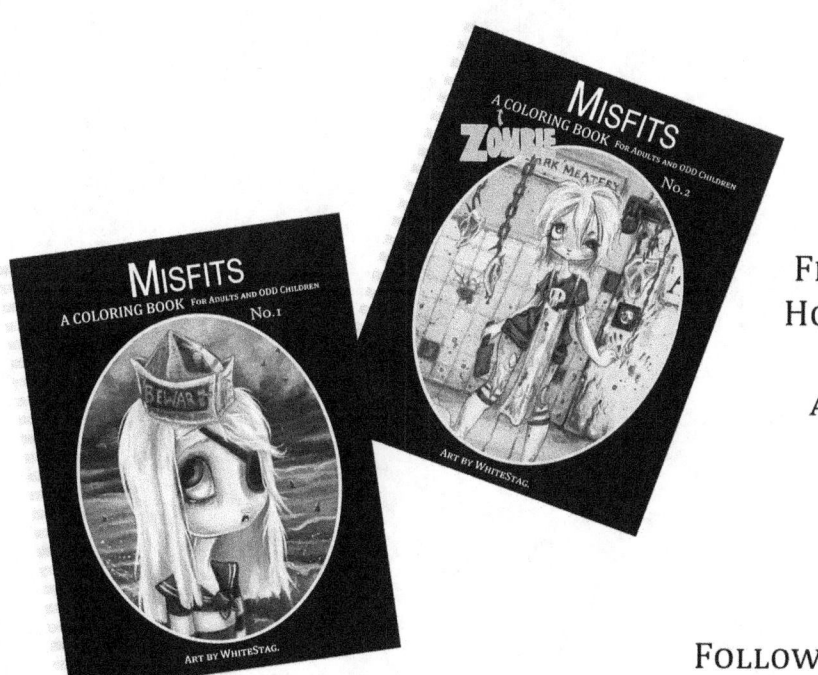

FIND VOL. 1 WITH A HEALTHY MEDLEY OF HOBO PRINCESSES, FAT CATS, SAILOR GIRLS +MORE
AND VOL. 2 A ZOMBIE ONLY EDITION ON AMAZON!

FOLLOW ME ON SOCIAL MEDIA FOR PREVIEWS AND RELEASES.

I LOVE TO SEE YOUR FINISHED IMAGES FEEL FREE TO SHARE YOUR COLORED IMAGES ON SOCIAL MEDIA! JUST MAKE SURE TO LIST THE BOOK YOU GOT IT FROM.

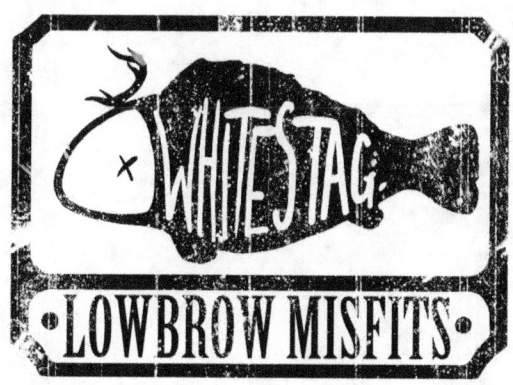

PRINTS, PAINTINGS AND MORE: WHITESTAG.ETSY.COM

| WHITESTAGART.COM | FACEBOOK.COM/TERRAFANTASYART |
| INSTAGRAM.COM/WHITESTAGART | TWITTER.COM/WHITESTAGART |

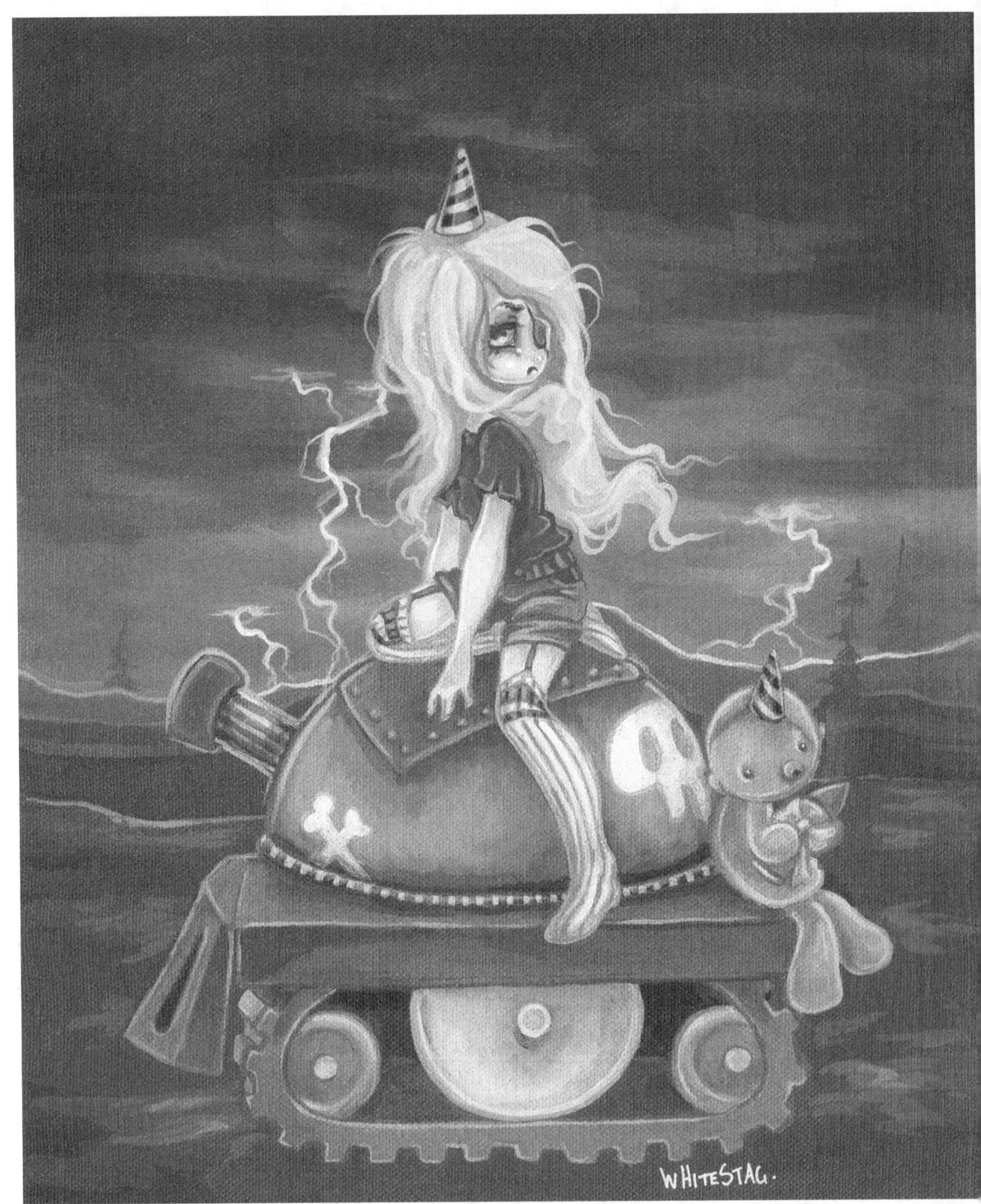

FOR ASTEL AND ANSLEY.